COVER DESIGN: JUSTIN KUO

COVER PHOTOGRAPHY: CHRIS PEACOCK

Copyright Steve Chua: Seek First International 2014   www.stevechua.net

ID ENCOUNTER WORKBOOK

TABLE OF CONTENTS

INTRODUCTION — 4

SESSION 1: CREATED FOR LOVE — 5
- REFLECTION QUESTIONS — 6
- SMALL GROUP QUESTIONS — 7
- PERSONAL MINISTRY EXERCISE — 8

SESSION 2: THE FALLEN IDENTITY AND THE POWER OF SHAME — 9
- REFLECTION QUESTIONS — 11
- SMALL GROUP QUESTIONS — 13
- PERSONAL MINISTRY EXERCISE — 14

SESSION 3: LIFE'S FOUR QUESTIONS — 17
- REFLECTION QUESTIONS — 19
- SMALL GROUP QUESTIONS — 21
- PERSONAL MINISTRY EXERCISE — 22

Copyright Steve Chua: Seek First International 2014   *www.stevechua.net*

SESSION 4: GOD'S PLAN FOR A HEALTHY IDENTITY   29

- REFLECTION QUESTIONS   31
- SMALL GROUP QUESTIONS   33
- PERSONAL MINISTRY EXERCISE   34

SESSION 5: THE TALE OF TWO TREES   36

- REFLECTION QUESTIONS   39
- SMALL GROUP QUESTIONS   41
- PERSONAL MINISTRY EXERCISE   42

SESSION 6: IDENTITY UNCOVERED   45

- REFLECTION QUESTIONS   49
- SMALL GROUP QUESTIONS   51
- PERSONAL MINISTRY EXERCISE   52

SESSION 7: IDENTITY RESTORED   55

- REFLECTION QUESTIONS   61
- SMALL GROUP QUESTIONS   63
- PERSONAL MINISTRY EXERCISE   64

ID ENCOUNTER WORKBOOK

INTRODUCTION

This ID Encounter workbook has been designed to accompany the media teaching series produced by Seek First International. Steve Chua has used his years of experience ministering to individuals to carefully craft this workbook to bring you into personal healing and identity breakthrough. Whether you choose to work through this series on an individual level or with others, this ministry tool will help you get the most out of the series and allow the Holy Spirit to work in your heart. Each section has notes that accompany the video teaching followed by questions to help you process and apply the truths into your life. Each section also includes personal ministry exercises that are designed to bring inner healing and release you into greater freedom.

This ID Encounter series was originally produced with small groups in mind. Personal healing is most effective when shared with others in a safe community. In an intimate group setting, those around us often can see things that as individuals we might overlook. In a context of love and security, this group environment can create greater intimacy and bonding, as members journey together to help each other discover God's original plan and design for their identity.

A PERSONAL WORD OF THANKS FROM STEVE CHUA

I believe this ID Encounter will bring many of God's children into their inheritance and God-given destiny. However this would not be possible if the following people had not been in my life. I want to thank my darling wife Barbara for the many years of unswerving belief in all that God was shaping in me. Your integrity, love and beauty have inspired me to be all that I am today. To my awesome kids: Joshua, Hannah, Abbey, Liz and Sophie you have taught me so much about how the Father loves. For my Mum and Dad, you have loved, interceded, blessed and supported me through my many ups and downs. To Gary and Garland Cheng, thank you for daring to dream and believe in this project. Finally I thank my Heavenly Father, whose love and grace allowed Jesus and the Holy Spirit to shape my orphan heart and transform me into a beloved son. All of this belongs to You and is for Your glory!

Copyright Steve Chua: Seek First International 2014 *www.stevechua.net*

SESSION 1: CREATED FOR LOVE

1. **INTRODUCTION**

2. **GOD IS LOVE**

    i. The nature of God is the glory of God.

    ii. God is love, and love requires relationship.

    iii. Love is expressed when you prefer, serve, promote and release THE OTHER.

3. **CREATED FOR INTIMACY: THE ORIGINAL DESIGN**

    i. The earth was created for man as a demonstration of God's love for man.

    ii. Man was created in the image and likeness of God (Genesis 1:26-27). It is when we reflect His image and likeness that relationship with Him can operate in its fullness.

    iii. The fullness of the glory of God flowed through Adam and woman (1 Corinthians 11:7).

    iv. Man was created spirit, soul and body (1 Thessalonians 5:23) in order to relate fully with God. Man was designed to receive and release God's glory.

    v. This is only possible if man and God are ONE through intimacy of relationship.

    vi. Man and woman were naked and not ashamed (Genesis 2:25). Transparency, vulnerability, innocence, security, and trust are all ingredients for intimacy.

    vii. Intimacy creates an environment and culture that freely receives and freely gives. This can only truly occur in an atmosphere of unconditional love and acceptance.

    viii. It is in the environment and encounter of unconditional love that true worth, value and significance are found.

SESSION 1: REFLECTION QUESTIONS - RECEIVING LOVE

1. On a Scale of 1-10 rate the following in regards to how you best receive love.
   (1 = Not at All & 10 = Amazingly)

	1	2	3	4	5	6	7	8	9	10
Positive words of encouragement and affirmation										
Quality time in relationship										
Physical touch and affection										
Receiving gifts (besides birthday & holidays)										
Acts of service (not dutiful expectations)										

2. On a Scale of 1-10 rate the following in regards to how your father demonstrated love to you.
   (1 = Not at All & 10 = Amazingly)

	1	2	3	4	5	6	7	8	9	10
Positive words of encouragement and affirmation										
Quality time in relationship										
Physical touch and affection										
Giving gifts (besides birthday & holidays)										
Acts of service (not dutiful expectations)										

3. On a Scale of 1-10 rate the following in regards to how your mother demonstrated love to you.
   (1 = Not at All & 10 = Amazingly)

	1	2	3	4	5	6	7	8	9	10
Positive words of encouragement and affirmation										
Quality time in relationship										
Physical touch and affection										
Giving gifts (besides birthday & holidays)										
Acts of service (not dutiful expectations)										

Copyright Steve Chua: Seek First International 2014   www.stevechua.net

SESSION 1: SMALL GROUP QUESTIONS

- What are the implications for us if we are made in the image and likeness of God?

- What are the keys that allow God to flow through your spirit, soul and body?

- What does love look like?

- How do you best receive love?

- How do you like to demonstrate or give love to another?

- What is unconditional love? What are the implications of receiving unconditional love?

> *"It is in the environment and encounter of unconditional love that true worth, value and significance are found."*

SESSION 1: PERSONAL MINISTRY EXERCISE

1. **INTRODUCTION:** Throughout this workbook, there are personal ministry exercise sections. These sections can be done on an individual basis or as a workshop within a small group. In a group setting, each section can be done as homework beforehand or as an exercise between teaching sessions.

2. **EXPLANATION:** These exercises are designed to resolve the conflicts of the heart that keep us from receiving our true identity. Before entering into each section of personal ministry, ask the Holy Spirit to reveal the hidden things of your heart (Psalm 139:23-24) – see prayer below. Then allow adequate time to reflect, process and listen to what words, memories, events and people are brought to your attention. If something comes to mind that is not obvious to you, ask the Holy Spirit as your counsellor (John 16:13) to give you insight and revelation (Ephesians 1:17). If you are doing this in a small group setting, allow people to share what the Holy Spirit is revealing to them. Encourage vulnerability in an environment of confidentiality, compassion, understanding and love. Avoid criticism and judgment for no one is without sin.

3. **APPLICATION:** To start, give the Holy Spirit permission to prepare your heart to be transformed. Pray the following prayer:

PERSONAL REFLECTION PRAYER

Lord Jesus,

You called the Holy Spirit 'the Spirit of Truth who would lead us into all truth.' Holy Spirit, as my counsellor and guide, I give You permission to search my heart, to know my heart, and to see if there's any unclean or hidden way within me. Give me a spirit of wisdom and revelation. Bring back to my mind any event, memory or word that has affected who I have become today. Lead me into all truth and take me deeper into Jesus, who is the way, the truth and the life. Let Your truth set me free to be all You created me to be.

In Jesus' name,

Amen.

SESSION 2: THE FALL AND THE POWER OF SHAME

1. **WHAT HAPPENED AT THE FALL?**

   "For all have sinned and fall short of the glory of God." (Romans 3:23)

   i. Sin is the action that separates us from God.
   ii. "You will be filled with shame instead of glory." (Habakkuk 2:16)
   iii. Shame is the consequence of sin that destroys our ability for intimacy with God.
   iv. After man sinned, he became aware of his shame. "There is something wrong with ME." Shame is the wrongness of being. As a result, we no longer consider others first but become self-focused (the flesh, self-life or sinful nature).
   v. Satan's primary objective is to destroy man's ability to relate intimately with God and others by destroying the core of his identity with shame.

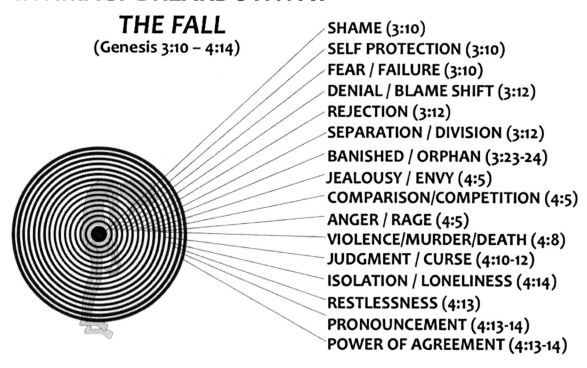

   vi. It was through relationship that glory flowed from God to man. The work of shame, destroys man's ability for intimacy (transparency, vulnerability, etc.) and prevents our inheritance of glory from flowing through our lives.

2. **JESUS CAME TO DEAL WITH THE POWER OF SIN AND SHAME IN ORDER TO RESTORE US BACK TO OUR ORIGINAL DESIGN.**

   Isaiah 61 prophesies the freedom the Messiah would bring.

   i. Preach good news to the poor. (Is 61:1)

   ii. Bind the broken hearted (restore to mint condition). (Is 61:1)

   iii. Bring deliverance (freedom and release for captives/prisoners). (Is 61:1)

   iv. Heal brokenness (comfort, restore, provide, replace). (Is 61:2-3)

   v. Deal with shame and restore our identity as "sons of glory." (Is 61:7)

3. **RESTORATION THROUGH THE CROSS**

   i. "Who for the joy set before Him endured the cross, scorning its shame, and sat down at the right hand of the throne of God." (Hebrews 12:2-3)

   ii. Jesus' encounter with our sin and shame in the garden of Gethsemane. *"If it is possible, take away this cup of suffering...Not My will, but Yours."* (Matthew 26:39)

   iii. Jesus' suffering identified with our suffering and shame.

   iv. Crucifixion and death dealt with the consequence of sin and shame.

   v. The temple curtain was torn in two - a picture of the restoration of access to God.

   vi. Why did Jesus have to die? To restore us back to relationship with God. (John 17:3)

SESSION 2: REFLECTION QUESTIONS - INTIMACY

1. On a Scale of 1-10 how would you rate the following in your life? (1 = Difficult & 10 = Very Easy)

	1	2	3	4	5	6	7	8	9	10
Do you find it easy to have deep relationships with others?										
Do you find it natural to be open and vulnerable with others?										
Is it easy for you to not worry about what others are thinking about you? (Especially those closest to you.)										
Do you trust others with things and information that are important or personal to you?										
Do you find it easy to fully commit to relationships?										
Do you find it easy to put others above your personal needs, wants and opinions?										
Is it comfortable for you not to be in control?										

2. If you find it hard to trust, what events or relationships in your life have caused your heart to be guarded?

3. If you find it hard to be open and vulnerable, what are you afraid would happen if you shared your weaknesses, mistakes and failures?

4. How do you see yourself in the light of your weaknesses, mistakes and failures?

SESSION 2: SMALL GROUP QUESTIONS

- What keeps people from intimacy and being able to relate with others?

- Shame causes us to hide ourselves – identify and define the types of shame that cause us to hide (e.g. failure, addiction, worthlessness etc.)?

- What do we do to cover our shame in order to keep people from getting too close to us?

- What did you learn about the work of Jesus on the cross that was new revelation to you?

> *"Sin is the action that separates us from God. Shame is the consequence that destroys intimacy with Him."*

SESSION 2: PERSONAL MINISTRY EXERCISE

PERSONAL ALIGNMENT: GIVING OVER CONTROL AND MAKING JESUS LORD OF YOUR LIFE

1. **EXPLANATION:** To be personally aligned with God in your spirit, soul and body, it is vital that you give up your need to be in control and allow Jesus to take control of every area of your life. This is a process of making Jesus, not just the Savior of your life, but also your LORD. This is done by relinquishing your control of every aspect of your life and giving control over to Jesus. As you take this step, it is vital that you understand that God's ways are better than your own. Healing for your past and your identity cannot come on your terms but on God's terms. Therefore His divine and created order must replace the disorder of self-protective and controlling life patterns. At the garden in Gethsemane Jesus modelled this to us when he prayed to God, "… not my will but yours be done." (Luke 22:42)

2. **REFLECTION:** For a few moments take time to ask the Holy Spirit to help you reflect on the aspects of your life that may not be aligned with God. These might be relationships, character issues, your time, finances, areas of independence etc. Look over the Lordship Prayer below to provoke your thoughts as you reflect. Write down the things that come to your heart as you spend time reflecting.

	Areas of my life where I need to make Jesus my LORD
1	
2	
3	
4	
5	
6	
7	
8	

3. **APPLICATION:** When you have finished reflecting, take time to pray the following prayer of Lordship, from your heart. If you need to add more personal specifics to the prayer, please be free to do so. The prayer below is simply an outline which you can personalize. After you have prayed this prayer, remember that the process of Lordship is a progressive work and not an instant transformation. Your prayer is a declaration of intent and will give permission for the Holy Spirit to begin His work of transformation in you.

LORDSHIP PRAYER

Lord Jesus,

I thank You for dying on the cross for me, and I accept You as my Saviour. Recognizing God's mercy and grace, I choose to offer my body, soul and spirit as a living sacrifice, holy and pleasing to You This is my spiritual act of worship. I choose to no longer conform to the pattern of this world, but to be transformed by the renewing of my mind. For then I will be able to test and approve what Your will is – Your good, pleasing and perfect will. (Romans 12:1-2)

I invite you now to be Lord of every area of my life, releasing my control and giving You full reign and possession of everything.

- *I ask You to be LORD of my SPIRIT:*
    - *LORD of my relationship with you;*
    - *LORD of my spiritual awareness and conscience;*
    - *LORD of my creativity and my spiritual gifts;*
    - *Lord of my worship;*
    - *LORD of my identity and who I am in you.*

- *I ask you to be LORD of my SOUL:*
    - *LORD of my MIND, my attitudes, my beliefs, my imagination, my dreams and all my thoughts;*
    - *LORD of my EMOTIONS, my expression of my feelings and all my reactions;*
    - *LORD of my WILL and all my decisions (conscious, subconscious and unconscious);*
    - *LORD of my defence mechanisms, coping mechanisms and my behaviour cycles.*

Copyright Steve Chua: Seek First International 2014   www.stevechua.net

- [ ] I ask you to be LORD of my BODY:

    - LORD of my physical health, exercise, rest, appearance and all my physical behavior;
    - LORD of my eyes and what I look upon;
    - LORD of my ears and everything I listen to;
    - LORD of my mouth and what I speak and eat;
    - LORD of my hands and all that I do and touch;
    - LORD of my feet and everywhere I go;
    - LORD of my sexuality and its expression.

- [ ] I ask you to be LORD of my PERSONAL LIFE:

    - LORD of my family (spouse, children, etc.) and my home;
    - LORD of my possessions, my needs (real and perceived), my finances;
    - LORD of my time, my work, my ministry, my pleasure;
    - LORD of my plans, my ambitions, my future, my destiny;
    - LORD of all my relationships.

Father, I say, "not my will but Yours be done" in my life. Thank You, Jesus, that You are LORD of all and my life is totally surrendered to You. Transform me, so my life reflect will reflect the glory of Who You are, LORD Jesus.

I declare and pray this in Jesus' name.

Amen.

SESSION 3: LIFE'S FOUR QUESTIONS

1. **INTRODUCTION**

2. **FOUR LIFE QUESTIONS WE NEED TO ANSWER**

    i. Who am I?

    ii. Why am I here?

    iii. Who can I trust?

    iv. Where do I fit?

3. **QUESTION 1: WHO AM I? IDENTITY**

    i. This is my <u>perception</u> of me.

    ii. It is about my value.

    iii. What am I worth?

    iv. Am I lovable?

    v. Am I acceptable just as I am?

4. **QUESTION 2: WHY AM I HERE? DESTINY**

    i. This is my perception of my function and reason for being here.

    ii. It is about finding significance.

    iii. It is about finding and realizing the call on my life.

    iv. It is about finding purpose.

    v. It is about having and being trusted with responsibility.

5. **QUESTION 3: WHO CAN I TRUST? <u>SECURITY</u>**

    i. This is my perception and trust in God, others and myself.

    ii. It is about my safety and protection.

    iii. Will anyone take care of and provide for me?

    iv. Am I willing to be vulnerable and trust another?

    v. Where will I go when I die?

6. **QUESTION 4: WHERE DO I FIT? <u>COMMUNITY</u>**

    i. This is my perception of family, marriage, home and society.

    ii. It is about finding an environment to discover identity, destiny and security.

    iii. It is about finding common unity with others about values, passion and purpose.

    iv. It is about thriving and contributing to affect and influence a greater body.

    v. Do I belong or am I alone on my journey of life?

> *"If you cannot answer the first question: 'Who am I?' then you will spend your life seeking value, worth, and significance in order to find your identity."*

SESSION 3: REFLECTION QUESTIONS – ID VALUE & WORTH

1. On a Scale of 1-10 rate what would give you the greatest sense of value, worth and significance from the following. (1 = Low Value & 10 = Greatest Value)

	1	2	3	4	5	6	7	8	9	10
Praise and affirmation from your father										
Praise and affirmation from your mother										
Praise and affirmation from a respected leader										
Personal success and achievement										
Recognition from your peers										
Having a position of responsibility										
Serving and helping others										
Having affection expressed and demonstrated towards you										
A significant person giving you their time										
Other:										

2. As you were growing up, how was value, worth and significance expressed to you by your parents?

3. Do you wrestle with insecurity and the fear of rejection, failure, disappointing others etc.? If the answer is yes, what are the events, circumstances or people that have caused or still cause fear and anxiety to rise within you.

4. Can you identify significant figures who have shamed or neglected you, making you feel worthless and insignificant? How have you dealt with the pain and rejection that came as a result of their words or actions?

SESSION 3: SMALL GROUP QUESTIONS

- How does society determine what has value, worth and significance?

- How did your family generate value, worth and significance for you?

- Where do you find your acceptance and how do you determine your worth?

- When do you feel most loved?

> *When Jesus gave His priceless life for you, He bought you back by paying the full price required to redeem you. That means in His eyes you are PRICELESS!"*

SESSION 3: PERSONAL MINISTRY EXERCISE

RESOLVING THE CONFLICTS OF THE HEART CAUSED BY OTHERS

1. **EXPLANATION:** Hurt is caused when we perceive that something or someone devalues us in our spirit, soul or body. When we have been hurt and damaged by others, it causes us to be offended, which will often lead to bitterness (Hebrews 12:15) and judgment. The Webster's Dictionary says that a judgment is the forming of a critical, authoritative opinion, perception or conclusion, as from circumstances presented to the mind. These judgments reinforce our sense of offense, which in turn acts as a "cancer to our soul" and keeps the trauma of the hurt locked up in our hearts. Every unresolved offense can have an adverse effect on what we believe others perceive about our identity (value, worth or significance) and can breed bitterness, anger, self-righteousness and rejection in our heart. The unresolved hurt will constantly remind us of our sense of devaluation and shame and will cause us to live out of self-protection and fear, rather than God's original design for our identity.

    To resolve these conflicts, Jesus gave us the principle of forgiveness. God designed forgiveness to resolve pain, to remove strongholds of the enemy from our lives, and to open the doors for reconciliation and restored relationships. Forgiveness is key to removing blockages to intimacy. When we choose to forgive from the heart, we "let go" of the person(s) who caused the offense. This means taking personal responsibility for our sin of judgment and releasing the offender(s) from any personal need of an apology, justice or vindication. Forgiveness is a choice not a feeling, and it needs to become a lifestyle, not just an isolated event. In fact, forgiveness is a daily process in some situations. Forgiveness is not always easy and can be costly. But remember, it cost Jesus the sacrifice of His life to forgive you. Forgiveness resolves the conflict of the heart and allows the hurt to be released as God brings His love and healing.

2. **REFLECTION:** For a few moments ask the Holy Spirit to help you reflect on the individuals in your life that you need to forgive. As names, faces and events come to mind, process the offender(s) and the actions that have devalued you. What did you perceive the hurtful action to say about your value, worth and significance in that moment? As you take these things into consideration, reflect on the pain and its consequences to your heart and life.

    You also may find that forgiveness needs to be extended to yourself. Often this is harder than forgiving others. In fact, if we tend to be performance-orientated, we often have little or no grace for ourselves. Reflect on ways you have blamed and judged yourself.

    Finally, it is possible you may have blamed or judged God in some way. When things don't work out, it is common for us to become angry at God. However, by judging Him, our unforgiveness creates a barrier between Him and us, and it becomes difficult to hear His voice and receive His love. Use the table following as a guide as you consider the areas in your life where judgments need to be released and forgiveness extended.

Copyright Steve Chua: Seek First International 2014   *www.stevechua.net*

FORGIVING MY PARENTS

NAME	EVENT OR ACTION THAT CAUSED MY OFFENSE (DIVORCE, ABUSE, NEGLECT, BROKEN TRUST, LACK OF AFFECTION ETC.)	WHAT DID THIS SAY ABOUT MY VALUE / WORTH / SIGNIFICANCE?
FATHER		

NAME	EVENT OR ACTION THAT CAUSED MY OFFENSE (DIVORCE, ABUSE, NEGLECT, BROKEN TRUST, LACK OF AFFECTION ETC.)	WHAT DID THIS SAY ABOUT MY VALUE / WORTH / SIGNIFICANCE?
MOTHER		

FORGIVING FAMILY MEMBERS
(GRANDPARENTS, UNCLES, AUNTS, SIBLINGS ETC.)

NAME	EVENT OR ACTION THAT CAUSED MY OFFENSE (DIVORCE, ABUSE, NEGLECT, FAVORITISM, BROKEN TRUST ETC.)	WHAT DID THIS SAY ABOUT MY VALUE / WORTH/ SIGNIFICANCE?

Copyright Steve Chua: Seek First International 2014

FORGIVING AUTHORITY FIGURES
(TEACHERS, COACHES, SPIRITUAL LEADERS, BOSSES ETC.)

NAME	EVENT OR ACTION THAT CAUSED MY OFFENSE (REJECTION, ABUSE, CONTROL, HUMILIATION, BROKEN TRUST ETC.)	WHAT DID THIS SAY ABOUT MY VALUE/WORTH/ SIGNIFICANCE?

FORGIVING OTHERS WHO HAVE HURT ME
(SPOUSE (EX), INTIMATE FRIENDS, BULLY, MUGGER, BUSINESS PARTNER ETC.)

NAME	EVENT OR ACTION THAT CAUSED MY OFFENSE	WHAT DID THIS SAY ABOUT MY VALUE / WORTH/ SIGNIFICANCE?

Copyright Steve Chua: Seek First International 2014   www.stevechua.net

FORGIVING MYSELF

EVENT OR ACTION THAT CAUSED MY SELF-BLAME	HOW DID THIS AFFECT MY SENSE OF VALUE /WORTH/SIGNIFICANCE?

RELEASING MY JUDGMENT AND BLAME TOWARD GOD

EVENT OR ACTION THAT CAUSED ME TO JUDGE AND BLAME GOD	WHAT DID THIS MAKE ME FEEL ABOUT GOD?

3. **APPLICATION:** When you have finished reflecting, take time to pray the prayer below from your heart. If you need to add personal specifics to the prayer, please be free to do so. The prayer below is simply an outline which you can personalize. As you forgive, audibly speak the name of the person. After you have prayed this prayer, remember that forgiveness is a progressive work. Remember that forgiveness is a lifestyle that will bring health to your soul and your relationships. Your prayer will give permission for the Holy Spirit to transform you.

PRAYER OF FORGIVENESS AND RELEASING OF JUDGMENTS

Lord Jesus,

Thank You for dying on the cross that I might be forgiven. As You have freely forgiven me of my sin, I now choose to forgive those who have hurt me. I choose to release the following people from my judgments towards them and I declare that I no longer need an apology, vindication or any form of justice. I release each of the following people to You, Lord Jesus, as the one, true judge.

(At this time, take a few moments to specifically name and release each individual the Holy Spirit has brought to your attention - see the following paragraph. Take time to see each person before you. As you forgive them, see yourself hand them over to Jesus.)

Therefore by an act of my will I forgive _____ (name the person/ yourself/ God) for _____ (name the action that hurt you), **and I release my judgment towards them.**

(After praying through your list, pray the following).

I release each of these people into the freedom of my forgiveness. I cancel any debt I feel I am owed and I ask You, Jesus, to cut off every ungodly influence between my heart and each of these people. I give You permission to pull out the bitter root of offense and hurt from me. I invite You, Holy Spirit, to renew my mind and heal the pain that was in my heart. I now choose to bless those who have cursed me.

(Take a few moments to release blessing and grace to those whom you have forgiven. Blessing cancels the curse that you have felt as a result of their wrongful actions.)

Thank You, Lord Jesus, that through Your work on the cross and by Your blood, I can release forgiveness and grace to others. Where I have been hurt, I now open my heart to trust again.

In Jesus name

Amen.

Copyright Steve Chua: Seek First International 2014   www.stevechua.net

SESSION 4: GOD'S PLAN FOR A HEALTHY IDENTITY

GOD'S PLAN FOR YOUR LIFE: God's plan is for you to have a healthy identity so that you can grow in relationship with Him and others.

1. **IDENTITY FORMATION - BIBLICAL FOUNDATION**

    i. You were known and chosen before time. (Eph. 1:4)

    ii. You are created in His image and likeness. (Gen 1:26)

    iii. You are His workmanship with a purpose and call. (Eph. 2:10)

    iv. You are unconditionally loved.

2. **IDENTITY DEVELOPMENT**

    i. Parents

    ii. Generational Blessings

    iii. Authority Figures

    iv. Cultural Blessings

    v. Significant Relationships

    vi. Life Experiences

3. **KEYS TO A GODLY AND HEALTHY IDENTITY - PROVISION**

    i. Love and nurture

    ii. Value, worth and significance

    iii. Affirmation and encouragement

    iv. Safety to fail, to grow and to learn

    v. Unconditional acceptance and belonging

    vi. Forgiveness and grace

    vii. Correction and discipline

    viii. Comfort and care

    ix. Security and protection

    x. Trust, consistency and integrity

Copyright Steve Chua: Seek First International 2014   www.stevechua.net

4. **IDENTITY DISCOVERY**

    i. I am loved - unconditionally.

    ii. I know that I am of value, worth and significance outside of anything I do. Priceless!

    iii. I am accepted just as I am.

    iv. I am secure and free to be me.

    v. I can open my heart for love and intimacy.

    vi. I am able to receive and give love.

"Failure is an event; it is not a person."

SESSION 4: REFLECTION QUESTIONS – ID PROVISION

1. On a Scale of 1-10 rate the following in regards to what you received growing up in your home for the first 16 years of your life. (1 = Non-Existent & 10 = Abundant)

	1	2	3	4	5	6	7	8	9	10
Nurture and physical affection										
Affirmation and encouragement										
Safety to fail, grow, learn and mature										
Unconditional acceptance and belonging										
Loving discipline and correction										
Forgiveness and grace										
Comfort and care in the midst of pain										
Protection										
Material provision										
Consistency (promises kept etc.)										
Freedom to share your opinion or disagreement										
Freedom to express your feelings										
Fun and laughter										
Freedom to explore, adventure and discover										
Freedom to be imaginative and creative										
Trust										

2. How close were you to your father and mother? Did you feel special to them? Explain your answer.

3. List the three areas that were lacking the most in your formative years. Because of the lack of receiving these blessings, how has it affected who you are today?

4. As a result, in what ways have you compensated for the lack of these blessings in your life (e.g. become driven for success or afraid to take risks etc.)?

SESSION 4: SMALL GROUP QUESTIONS

- What should home be?

- What are the ingredients for a healthy home?

- In what ways did your home strengthen or weaken your identity?

- Growing up what events or people either blessed your identity or had a negative impact upon your identity?

> "Home is where you story begins."

SESSION 4: PERSONAL MINISTRY EXERCISE

REMOVING THE CONSEQUENCES OF SIN FROM OUR LIVES.

1. **EXPLANATION:** Without Jesus, sin will separate us from God. Sin is the choice that we make to disobey or rebel against God's order of blessing for our lives. The consequence of sin brings us into shame, which destroys our relationship with God and others. That shame causes guilt to be established in our hearts and leads us into self-condemnation, self-judgment, and then self-rejection and self-hatred. As a result, we no longer see the image of God within us, but a distorted and shameful image. This shame then causes us pain that we will either seek to escape or to comfort. Inevitably, if we find something that helps us to run away from the pain or that provides a false comfort for the pain, we can become addicted to it. Therefore, sin gives the enemy a foothold (Ephesians 4:27) to exercise his power and authority over our lives.

    The gift of repentance removes the judgment and condemnation from our lives. It allows us to bring the darkness of our hearts into the light. It activates and releases grace, so that we can turn from our ungodly, self-destructive mindsets. This is a two-step process of confession and repentance. 1 John 1:9 says, " If we confess our sins, he is faithful and just and will forgive us our sins and purify us from all unrighteousness." Confession of our sin means that we take responsibility for what we have done to ourselves and to others. Repentance means that we turn from our ungodly behaviour and ask the Holy Spirit to transform our propensity to sin in that area. This process is the first step in removing the devil's foothold in your life.

2. **REFLECTION:** For a few moments ask the Holy Spirit to help you reflect on situations and choices you have made that still bring you a sense of remorse, regret, guilt and condemnation. Write down the things that come to your heart that you need to confess (take responsibility for) and repent from (turn away from).

	AREAS OF MY LIFE THAT I NEED TO CONFESS AND REPENT FROM
1	
2	
3	
4	
5	
6	
7	

Copyright Steve Chua: Seek First International 2014   www.stevechua.net

3. **APPLICATION:** When you have finished reflecting, take time to pray the following prayer from your heart. If you need to add personal specifics to the prayer, please be free to do so. The prayer is simply an outline which you can personalize. After you have prayed this prayer, remember that repentance is not an isolated event, but a lifestyle to keep us walking in God's light. When we are in the light, we can begin to see the glory of who God created us to be.

   Additionally, James 5:16 says "...confess your sins to each other and pray for each other so that you may be healed". Therefore, you may be led to share and confess your sin to a spiritually mature, trusted friend. It is good to clear your conscience and be forgiven.

PRAYER OF CONFESSION AND REPENTANCE

Lord Jesus,

Thank You for dying that I might be forgiven of my sin. Your Word says that if I confess my sin, You will forgive me of my sin and cleanse me from all unrighteousness. (1 John 1:9) Therefore, I take responsibility for my wrongful actions. I confess that I have sinned in thought, in word, and in deed. So by an act of my will, I repent and confess my sins to You.

(At this time, take a few moments to specifically confess the sins that the Holy Spirit has brought to your attention).

Thank You, Lord Jesus, that through Your work on the cross and by Your blood, You remove my sin and cleanse me whiter than the snow. I now ask You to remove every ungodly influence or consequence that has given Satan a foothold in my life. Break every curse that has affected me, and those that I love. Thank You for the grace and mercy that You have given to me, and that I no longer live under condemnation of these sins (Romans 8:1). So, I release my guilt, my self-condemnation, my self-judgment, self-hatred and self-rejection to You. I now choose to receive the mercy and the grace that You lavish on me.

Thank You that You have forgiven me and I now choose to forgive myself. I choose to turn from my ungodly mindsets, choices and behavior and walk from darkness into Your light.

In Jesus' name,

Amen

SESSION 5: THE TALE OF TWO TREES

SATAN'S PLAN FOR YOUR LIFE: Satan's plan is to destroy intimacy and relationship with God and with others by destroying YOU!

1. **UNGODLY IDENTITY DEVELOPMENT**

   Satan is not a creator and must work within God's created order. Therefore he uses the same six areas that were meant for blessing to bring curse.

   i. Parental Dysfunction

   ii. Generational Curses

   iii. Abusive Authority

   iv. Cultural Bondage

   v. Broken Relationships

   vi. Traumatic Experiences

   vii. Genesis 3:10 – 4:14

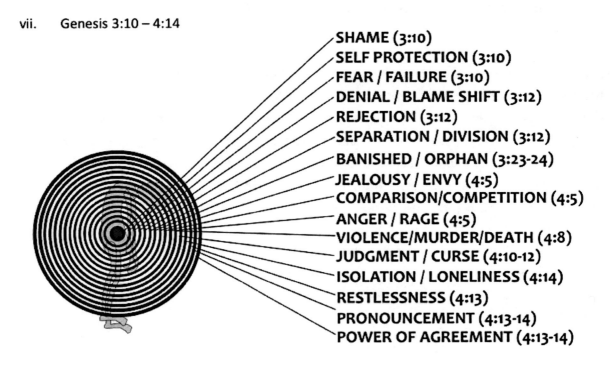

SHAME (3:10)
SELF PROTECTION (3:10)
FEAR / FAILURE (3:10)
DENIAL / BLAME SHIFT (3:12)
REJECTION (3:12)
SEPARATION / DIVISION (3:12)
BANISHED / ORPHAN (3:23-24)
JEALOUSY / ENVY (4:5)
COMPARISON/COMPETITION (4:5)
ANGER / RAGE (4:5)
VIOLENCE/MURDER/DEATH (4:8)
JUDGMENT / CURSE (4:10-12)
ISOLATION / LONELINESS (4:14)
RESTLESSNESS (4:13)
PRONOUNCEMENT (4:13-14)
POWER OF AGREEMENT (4:13-14)

2. **THERE WERE TWO TREES IN THE GARDEN**

   In the scriptures, names are critical for understanding and revelation.

   i. The Tree of Life

   ii. The Tree of the Knowledge of Good and Evil

3. **TREE OF LIFE**

   <u>Psalm 1:1-3</u>

   *"Blessed is the man who does not walk in the counsel of the wicked or stand in the way of sinners or sit in the seat of mockers. But his delight is in the law of the LORD, and on his law he meditates day and night. **He is like a tree** planted by streams of water which **yields its fruit in season** and whose **leaf does not wither. Whatever he does prospers."***

   <u>Jeremiah 17:7-8</u>

   *"But **blessed** is the man **who trusts in the LORD**, whose **confidence** is in him. **He will be like a tree** planted by the water that sends out its roots by the stream. It **does not fear** when heat comes; its **leaves are always green**. It has **no worries** in a year of drought and **never fails to bear fruit."***

4. **TREE OF THE KNOWLEDGE OF GOOD AND EVIL**

   <u>Jeremiah 17:5-6</u>

   *"**Cursed** is the one who **trusts in man**, who depends on **flesh for his strength** and whose heart turns away from the LORD. He will be like a **bush in the wastelands**; he will **not see prosperity** when it comes. He will **dwell in the parched places** of the desert, in a salt land **where no one lives."***

   <u>Luke 6:43-45</u>

   *"No good tree bears bad fruit, nor does a bad tree bear good fruit. Each tree is recognized by its own fruit…The good man brings good things out of **the good stored up in his heart**, and the evil man brings evil things out of the **evil stored up in his heart**. For out of the overflow of his heart his mouth speaks. "*

5. UNDERSTANDING YOUR TREE

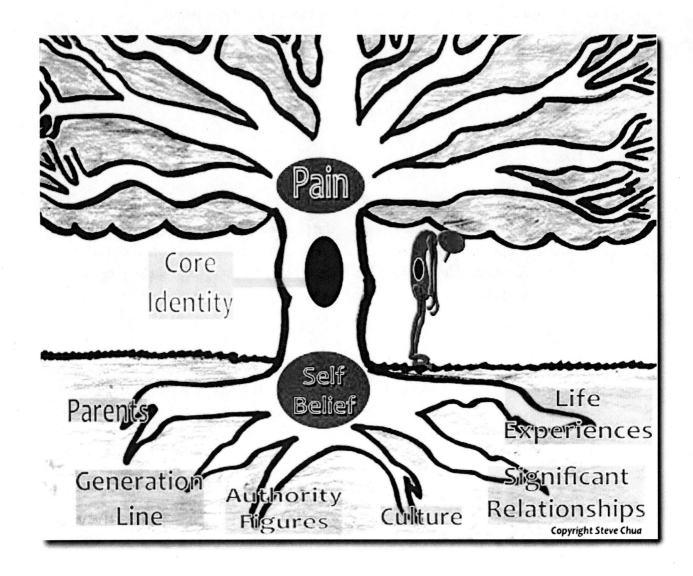

SESSION 5: REFLECTION QUESTIONS – IDENTITY ROOTS

1. On a scale of 1-10 how have your experiences and expectations of the following affected your sense of self worth and value?

    (1= Negatively impacted my identity & 10 = Positively impacted my identity)

Close Family	1	2	3	4	5	6	7	8	9	10
Father										
Mother										
Spouse										
Brother(s)										
Sister(s)										
Paternal Grandfather										
Paternal Grandmother										
Maternal Grandfather										
Maternal Grandmother										
Other Specific Relatives										
Name:										
Name:										
Name:										
Other Significant Relationships										
Name:										
Name:										
Name:										
Significant Authority Figures										
Name:										
Name:										
Name:										
Cultural Expectations										
Education:										
Public Image:										
Religion:										
Family Values:										
Significant Life Experiences										
Event:										
Event:										
Event:										
Event:										

2. Identity is formed and developed by six primary areas (parents, generation line, authority figures, significant relationships, culture and personal life experiences). Which of these 6 areas has blessed your identity the most? Recall the specific ways this area has given you value, worth and significance to your identity.

3. Which of these 6 areas have negatively affected your identity the most? Recall the specific ways this area has negatively affected your value, worth and significance in your identity.

SESSION 5: SMALL GROUP QUESTIONS

- How have each of the six roots impacted your identity?

- How have each of the six roots impacted your sense of purpose and hope for the future?

- How have each of the six roots impacted your sense of security and trust in others?

- How have each of the six roots impacted your involvement in community and your sense of belonging?

> "...They will be called oaks of righteousness, a planting of the LORD for the display of His splendour."
> (Isaiah 61:3)

SESSION 5: PERSONAL MINISTRY EXERCISE

FREEDOM FROM THE INFLUENCE OF UNGODLY RELATIONSHIPS

1. **EXPLANATION:** God created relationships to be transformational. His intention is that, through love, our relationships would release life and blessing to one another. Every relationship has the ability to impact our spirit, soul and body. When relationships operate as God intended, we form a RELATIONSHIP BOND. The word bond gives us a sense of something that is inseparable, strongly joined. When this bond is healthy, it releases value, love and significance into our lives.

   However, when a relationship operates out of the fruits of shame, it becomes unhealthy. Instead of releasing the flow of blessing, the enemy uses unhealthy relationships to bring curses into our lives and to bring us into BOND-AGE. Betrayals, rejection, fear, control, anger all negatively affect and potentially damage our soul. The ungodly actions of others cause us to self-protect and thus impair our ability to make healthy decisions in relationships and life. These ungodly RELATIONSHIP BONDAGES (sometimes known as "soul ties") keep us bound to the trauma caused by the unhealthy relationship. Even years after the event or association we may still carry the scars and wounds that were caused by ungodly relationships. In this section, you will work on freeing yourself from the curse of ungodly relationships.

2. **REFLECTION:** As you examine the six roots of the tree diagram, you may discover that you have received curses rather than blessings through some of your relationships. Over the past few sessions, you have had opportunity to forgive those who have hurt you and to repent of wrong actions you may have inflicted on others. That is the groundwork needed to begin to free yourself from the ungodly influences that Satan has been using to destroy your identity.

   In the following table, take time to consider the significant relationships that have hurt you and deprived you of the blessing and love you should have received. Identify the pain by which the enemy has bound you through these ungodly relationship bondages. As you identify the pain caused by these relationships, you can give yourself permission to let the trauma go. You can separate the ungodly influence of those relationships from impacting your soul. And in turn, you can release and bless those who have cursed you.

IDENTIFYING UNGODLY RELATIONSHIPS

NAME THE UNGODLY RELATIONSHIP (PARENT, BOSS, TEACHER, SEXUAL PARTNER ETC.)	LIST THE EVENT, ATTITUDE, ACTION OR WORDS THAT HAVE CURSED ME (ABUSE, REJECTION, BETRAYAL, SEX ETC.)	WHAT ATTITUDES OR BEHAVIOR HAVE I ADOPTED AS A RESULT OF THIS? (ISOLATION, PERFORMANCE, FEAR ETC.)

3. **APPLICATION.** Now that you have identified the key relationships that have cursed you, you can now break the ungodly ties and release the pain you have held onto. (If you have not forgiven the people on your list, take time to release your judgments of them. Refer the Prayer of Forgiveness and Releasing Judgments on page 28). Use the prayer below to pray to release yourself from the bondage with those who have negatively affected you. In addition, there will also be an opportunity to break the ties and cancel the curses that have been in operation your life. Pray this prayer through for each of the ungodly relationships you listed on the previous table.

Please note that some relationships have a mixture of good and bad. For example, we want to honor our parents, but we recognize that they are not perfect. When you break the ungodly bondages, honor any good there might be in those relationships, but remove the ungodly influences that undermine the health of the relationship. (1 Thessalonians 5:21-22)

PRAYER TO BREAK THE INFLUENCES OF UNGODLY RELATIONSHIPS

In the name of Jesus,

Having repented for my sins and forgiven those who have affected me in ungodly ways, I now take the sword of the Spirit and I break the relationship bondage (soul tie) between _____ (Name the ungodly relationship) and myself. I ask You, Jesus, to extract every negative influence of ... (Name the ungodly relationship) that has impacted my spirit, soul (mind, will, and emotions) and body. I renounce all co-dependency, ungodly pleasure and control that has been in operation between us. I break the power of every curse that the enemy has been using against me as a result of this relationship. I bless _____ (Name the ungodly relationship) and honor all that is godly between us. However I now specifically break the following consequences (curses) that have negatively affected me: _____ (List the ungodly effects).

Holy Spirit, I invite You into the pain and trauma that has kept me in bondage, and I ask you to take the hurt and free my emotions. Deliver me from any evil consequence as I close the door to the enemy's schemes in my life. I now put the cross of Jesus between _____ (Name the ungodly relationship) and myself, so that the enemy can no longer use this relationship to curse me.

In pray this in the mighty name of Jesus.

Amen.

SESSION 6: IDENTITY UNCOVERED

1. **SATAN'S PLAN FOR YOUR IDENTITY**

    i. Satan seeks to destroy your "core identity" with lies.

    ii. The lies are established through the "POWER OF AGREEMENT."

    iii. Power of agreement is the relinquishing of your free will choice by choosing to agree with Satan's lie(s) about who you are.

    iv. This agreement becomes a curse on your identity which will keep you from God's blessing.

    v. These lies form "core beliefs" within your identity which are based on shame and fear.

    vi. Negative "core beliefs" will produce fear-based behaviors which form ungodly, self-destructive coping mechanisms.

    vii. As a result, these negative "core beliefs" will keep you from the transforming truth of God's Word and the blessing of being His child.

EXAMPLES OF NEGATIVE "CORE IDENTITY" BELIEFS

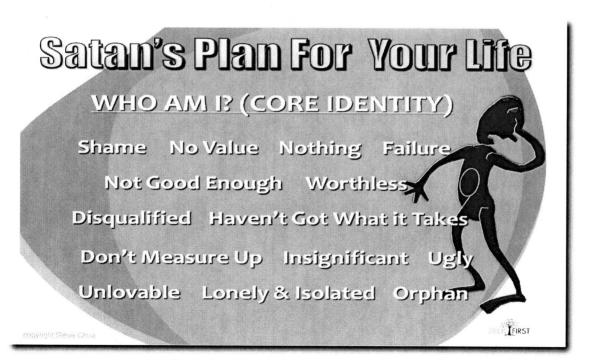

2. **SATAN'S PLAN TO MAINTAIN AND REINFORCE YOUR NEGATIVE "CORE IDENTITY"**

   Satan's plan is to destroy the soul (mind, emotions and will) in order to keep you from nurturing and growing your human spirit.

   i. **MIND:** Satan seeks to continually feed you lies to keep you from believing God's plan for your identity. His authority and power is established over you if these lies become "strongholds" within your mind.

   ii. **EMOTIONS:** Satan will use traumatic experiences and challenging circumstances to keep you from resolving negative emotions. Satan seeks to keep our emotional store full of negativity and conflict. Continual feelings of pain, fear, rejection, failure etc. will keep you distracted with circumstance rather than resolving identity issues within your mind. Therefore, these emotions will cause you to interpret (filter) your natural circumstances, often reinforcing your negative "core beliefs."

   iii. **WILL:** These negative lies established in the mind, coupled with the recycling of negative feelings, will begin to determine the choices and actions you make. This will often lead to compulsive, self-protective and self-destructive behavior.

EXAMPLES OF FRUIT PRODUCED AS A RESULT OF AN UNGODLY CORE IDENTITY

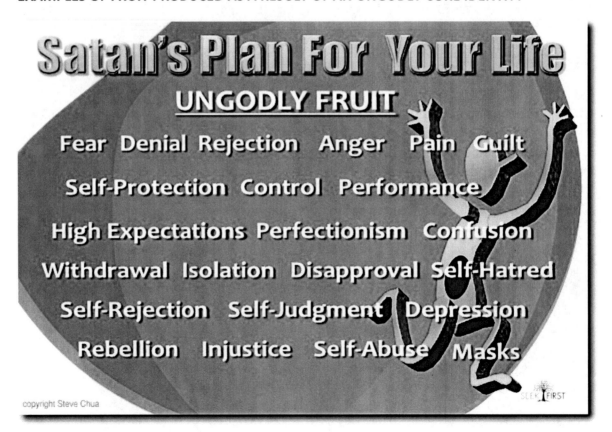

Copyright Steve Chua: Seek First International 2014

3. **DEVELOPMENT OF SELF-DESTRUCTIVE COPING AND DEFENSE MECHANISMS**

    i. As a result of the continual feelings of shame based out of the negative core identity, the soul begins to find coping mechanisms to deal with the pain. Also defense mechanisms will be formed to try to control the environment to keep pain from recurring.

    ii. These coping mechanisms will cause you to seek comfort or escape from your internal negative reality.

    iii. Once a mechanism is found, addictive behaviour may begin to manifest.

    iv. Defense mechanisms will always seek to protect you (either fight or flight) from any perceived danger that would expose your shame-based identity.

4. EFFECTIVE HEALING FOCUSES ON THE CORE IDENTITY AND NOT THE MANIFESTED FRUIT

i. Often we focus on the fruit or coping mechanisms as the problem, believing that our behaviour (such as addiction, anger, etc.) is the cause of our internal conflict.

ii. However the question that needs to be asked is why do we behave this way? What is this behavior comforting or protecting? What are we trying to escape from? What do we not want to face?

iii. As we look at the tree diagram, the root system is only a part of the problem. It is true that we have been formed by what has been fed through the root system. However dealing with the roots does not change who we are.

iv. The roots and fruits are external factors to the internal (core) self-belief. It is easier to blame something or someone than to take ownership for ourselves. That is the fruit and behavior of our shame.

v. We need to realise that a tree does not grow from its roots. Roots come from a seed. This seed is who we are, created before the foundation of the world. The seed is what brings life to the tree.

vi. The seed is our core identity: what I believe about my value, worth, and significance.

vii. What we believe in our core identity will create filters by which we interpret our relationships and circumstances. These will affect our choices, behavior, character, and ultimately our destiny.

viii. Simply bringing counsel, prayer ministry, inner healing and deliverance to the fruit or roots will not change one's core identity. That's not to say that these ministry tools are not important. The process of personal ministry often resolves external conflicts that clear the ground to get to the heart.

ix. Our Heavenly Father has sent us the Holy Spirit to be the Spirit of Truth. He desires for us to encounter a tangible transforming relationship of love with Him. It is the truth that sets us free. When we encounter a Holy Spirit breathed revelation, it transforms and renews our mind. It can break the strongholds of our futile thinking and restore who we were created to be.

x. One word from God is better than tens of thousands of hours of human reason and counselling.

SESSION 6: REFLECTION QUESTIONS – UNGODLY FRUIT

1. On a scale of 1-10 how much do you struggle with the following?
   (1 = Not at All & 10 = Highly)

	1	2	3	4	5	6	7	8	9	10
Insecurity and fear										
Failure										
Rejection										
Defensiveness (self-protection) and denial										
Blame-shifting and making excuses										
Jealousy and envy										
Constant comparison										
Competitiveness										
Need to prove yourself										
Perfectionism										
Performance orientation (high expectations)										
Rebellion against authority										
Critical and judgmental of others										
Anger										
Rage and aggressive behavior (violence)										
Self-judgment (negative criticism against self)										
Self-hatred (self-condemnation)										
Guilt										
Sadness										
Anxiety										
Depression										
Suicidal thoughts										
Isolation and loneliness										
Lust & sexual temptation										
Addictive behavior										
Obsessive behavior										
Greed or hoarding										
Need to control										
Being disapproved of										
People-pleasing (difficult to say no)										
Apathy (no point trying)										
Procrastination										
Wearing mask to adapt to different situations										

Copyright Steve Chua: Seek First International 2014   www.stevechua.net

2. When facing stress, anxiety, pressure or pain, to what do you turn to help you cope, comfort or escape from the conflict that you are facing?

3. What CORE identity beliefs do you have that may sabotage God's best for your life? Start with I am... (For example: I am a failure, I am disqualified, I am not good enough etc.).

SESSION 6: SMALL GROUP QUESTIONS

- What causes you fear and insecurity?

- What causes you the most stress and anxiety?

- What are some of the core negative "I am" statements that you have believed about yourself?

- How have these core statements affected your behavior and decision making process?

> "There is no fear in love. But perfect love drives out all fear...The one who fears is not made perfect in love."
> (I John 4:18)

SESSION 6: PERSONAL MINISTRY EXERCISE

UNCOVERING THE SHAME UPON YOUR IDENTITY

1. **EXPLANATION:** In this section you will begin to identify your core identity beliefs. It is these fixed core beliefs that will often sabotage the blessing God intended for your life. As you delve into the areas of your subconscious mind, you will begin to see behaviors and attitudes that produce ungodly fruit. It is important to understand what motivates your choices. If they come from a place of shame, then your choices will often be self-protective and self-centered. The result will keep you in a performance trap and bring dysfunction into your relationships. God's intention is that love would be the motivating force of our identity. So, instead of living to fill a love deficit, you are free to overflow with love to those around you, bringing and releasing love wherever you go.

2. **REFLECTION:** As you reflect on your life journey and the different people and events that have shaped what you fundamentally believe about your value, worth and significance, take time to create your own "Identity Tree" by using the worksheet found in this section. Try to be as specific and detailed as possible.

    <u>**A Guide to completing the Identity Tree:**</u>

    i. Consider how the six roots have acted or spoken negatively into your value, worth and significance. Focus on each root and list any negative effects on your life. For example: rejection, abandonment, neglect, physical abuse etc.

    ii. Determine what message(s) you received from these roots about who you are (your self-belief). For example: I am not good enough; everything is my fault; I am a failure etc. List these self-beliefs in the box on the left.

    iii. List the pain that these beliefs have caused you in the box on the right. For example: disapproval, self-hatred, anger, insecurity, betrayal etc.

    iv. Finally, list the fruit of what your life has produced as a result of the pain and self-belief. Remember we look to escape or comfort our pain. For example: Addictions (sex, drugs etc.), control, driven personality, depression, perfectionism etc.

IDENTITY TREE WORKSHEET

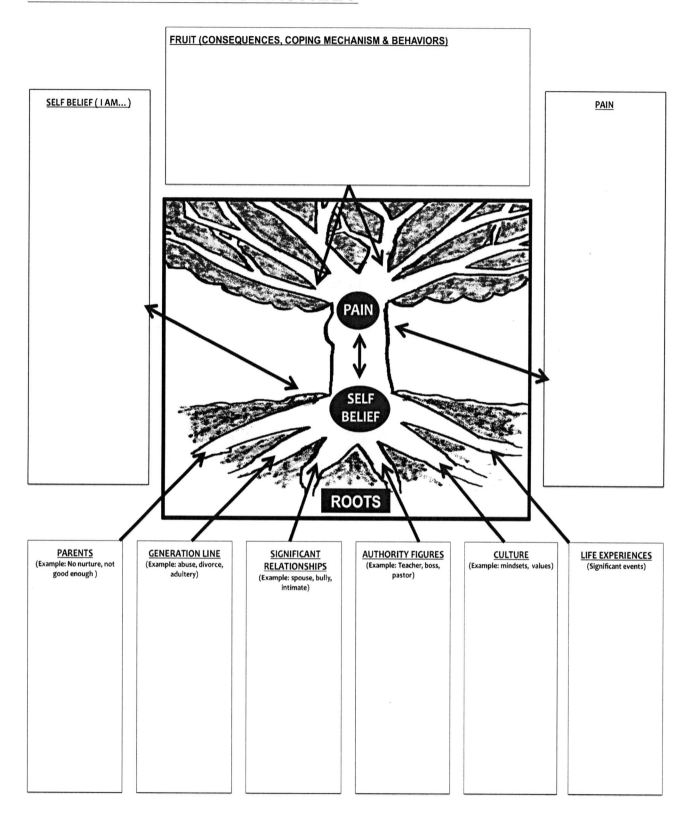

3. **APPLICATION:** Once you have completed the Identity Tree worksheet you should begin to understand why you wrestle with some of the personal issues that you have. The roots will show you the people and events that have negatively affected your core identity. Remember, God's intention is that blessing should flow to you through these six roots. However, many times we end up receiving negative messages that impact what we believe about ourselves.

   The self-belief statements that you subconsciously have agreed with create emotional reactions of pain. The combination of negative beliefs and emotional pain then form mindsets about your core identity. These mindsets and your negative emotions affect your personality, choices, relationships and future. As a result, negative fruit emerges from these mindsets. Mechanisms of escape or false comfort are then formed to compensate for or cover the pain that is felt within your core.

   As you look at your Identity Tree, you will begin to see how the enemy has attempted to destroy your identity. Now that you can see his plan, you can begin to reverse all that he has done, and allow the full work of the cross to bring healing and freedom to your heart. In the following sections we will begin to deal with your pain and your negative core beliefs.

   In preparation, it is important for the Holy Spirit to confirm to you what has been presented through the Tree. In the coming days, take time to observe your reactions and responses to the various situations and relationships that are presented to you. Ask the Holy Spirit to show you the motivations behind your conversations, choices and actions. (Are you trying to impress? To cover a mistake? Wanting to be liked?) In addition, if you find yourself reacting in anger or rejection in the midst of a conflict, ask the Holy Spirit what you perceived was being projected about your value, worth and significance. To help you, pray the following prayer to prepare your heart for freedom.

   A PRAYER FOR THE HOLY SPIRIT TO SEARCH YOUR HEART

   Lord Jesus,

   You came to set the captives free. So, Holy Spirit, I give You permission to show me the truth concerning the condition of my heart. Confirm the shame that has been hiding within. Bring to light everything of darkness, so that Your truth can set me free.

   I pray this in Jesus' name.

   Amen.

SESSION 7: IDENTITY RESTORED

1. **LEARNING TO COVER UP SHAME**

    i. As a result of the fall, our natural reaction to our shame is to hide ourselves.

    ii. If we have negative beliefs in our core identity, then it is natural for us to not display what we believe to be our shameful self.

    iii. Therefore, the result of shame ("There is something wrong with me.") causes us to ask ourselves "What must I do to make something right with me?"

    iv. Our shame makes us unacceptable and causes us to move into self-rejection.

    v. The questions become "What will make me acceptable?" and "What must I do or who do I need to become to find acceptance?"

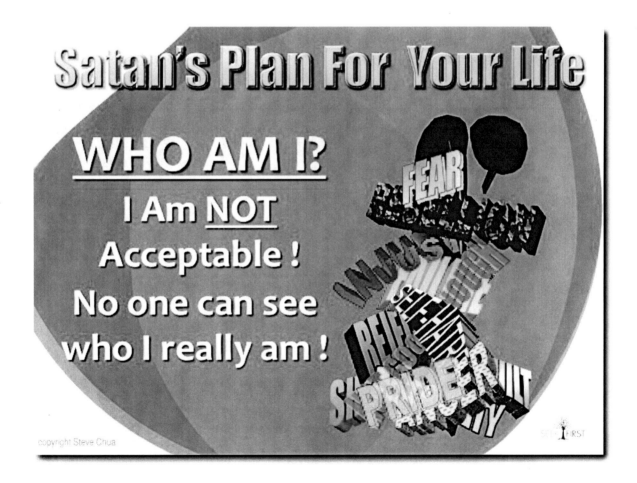

2. **THE CREATION AND EXPECTATION OF THE SUPER IMAGE**

   i. In order to hide our shame, we often create an outward image built on the expectation of what we believe will make us acceptable.

   ii. These expectations often seem rational and good. So we form an image that we believe will find acceptance for ourselves.

   iii. These expectations are often created out of either what we believe we are lacking in ourselves or what the culture or environment deems as acceptable.

   iv. High expectations are created, and we spend our time trying to meet what we perceive to be the expectations of others, believing that these will overcome the shame that we feel internally (subconsciously).

   v. This super image is based on performance, which we try to project to those around us, believing that it will bring value, worth, praise and love to our identity.

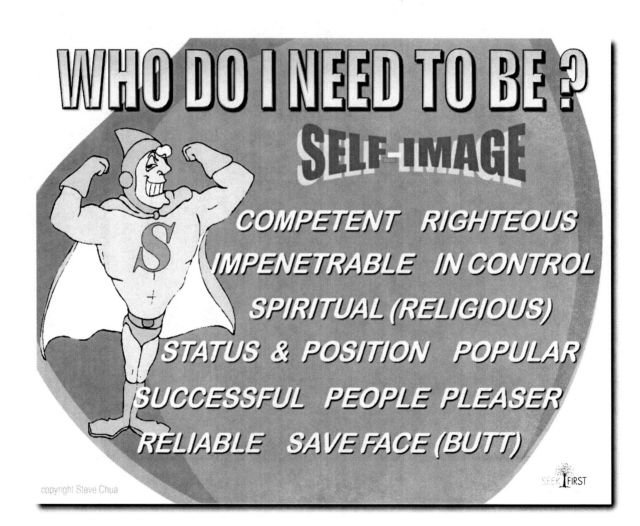

Copyright Steve Chua: Seek First International 2014   www.stevechua.net

3. **FORMATION OF AN ALTERNATIVE IMAGE**

   i. We all have a list of subconscious super-expectations that we hold over ourselves.

   ii. However, for some, these expectations reinforce our shame because we have set impossible goals for ourselves.

   iii. As a result, a different self-protective image is projected. This will come in the form of FLIGHT or FIGHT.

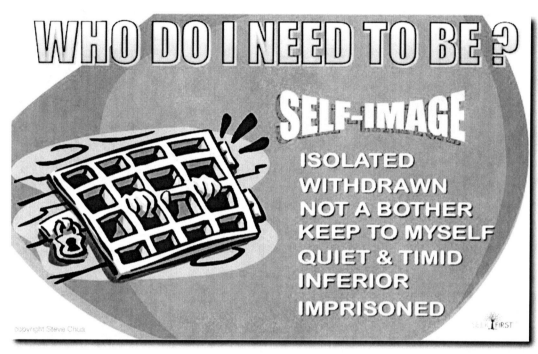

4. SAVING YOURSELF THROUGH THE FALSE IMAGE

i. The formation of our false self-image is caused as a result of our perceived shame and consequential lack of value, worth, love and significance.

ii. As a result, we often find ourselves performing to find our worth, acceptance and love.

iii. One misconception is that if we have a revelation of God's acceptance or the acceptance of others, this will overcome our own rejection. However, this is not true! If we believe that we are not acceptable to ourselves then we will never believe that we are good enough to be accepted by others.

iv. When I am able accept myself, then God and others will be able to accept me!

v. Our sense of acceptance comes when we are able to perform to meet our expectation for self-worth and acceptance. We believe, "If I am able to meet my goals and expectations, then I have made it".

vi. Our desire is for others to see our self-created super-image because that is what we want to become.

vii. However, this leads us to believe that God wants us to be good, successful, perfect people so that He can bless us.

viii. Therefore, we project our performance image to God for acceptance. However, His response to the image is "I never knew you!"

Matthew 7:18-23

"A good tree cannot bear bad fruit, and a bad tree cannot bear good fruit. Every tree that does not bear good fruit is cut down and thrown into the fire. Thus, by their fruit you will recognize them. Not everyone who says to me, 'Lord, Lord,' will enter the kingdom of heaven, but only he who does the will of my Father who is in heaven. Many will say to me on that day, 'Lord, Lord, did we not prophesy in your name, and in your name drive out demons and perform many miracles?' Then I will tell them plainly, 'I never knew you. Away from me, you evildoers!'

x. Our performance, position, etc. brings us a false sense of value. Our worth becomes based purely on what we do and not who we are.

xi. Therefore, failure and mistakes prevent us from having grace for ourselves because our performance has become our identity.

xii. However, subconsciously we believe that by meeting these expectations we are proving our worth and ridding ourselves of our shame. As a result, we are trying to save ourselves through a righteousness of our own.

Luke 9:23-25

"If anyone would come after me, he must deny himself and take up his cross daily and follow me. For whoever wants to save his life will lose it, but whoever loses his life for me will save it. What good is it for a man to gain the whole world, and yet lose or forfeit his very self?

5. **TEARING DOWN THE IDOL OF SELF**

    i. This self-image is a false identity, created by the self and is not in the image of God. In search of personal value, the pursuit to become this image becomes all-consuming.

    ii. The scripture speaks of graven images or idols that are man-made.

    iii. Idols are an abomination to the LORD, and we are commanded to tear these images down from their high places.

    iv. Self-idolatry is sin and keeps you from the grace of God and His blessing to bring true restoration and healing to your authentic self. (Jonah 2:8)

    v. By maintaining the false image, you reject the one that God knew, chose and created before the foundation of the world.

    vi. Therefore the key to breakthrough is learning to accept ourselves, despite our own imperfections. When we are able to do this, then God is able to bring His healing and restoration to our identity.

> *"Therefore, if anyone is in Christ, he is a new creation, the old has gone, the new has come."*
> *(2 Corinthians 5:17)*

SESSION 7: REFLECTION QUESTIONS – PERFORMANCE

1. On a Scale of 1-10 how would you rate your response to the following?
   (1=Not at All & 10 = Very Much)

	1	2	3	4	5	6	7	8	9	10
How driven are you to succeed?										
How important has it been to you to have a title or letters after your name?										
How important has it been for you to be noticed and seen?										
How important is it to you that you have to be RIGHT?										
How much do you compare yourself to others to see if you measure up?										
How difficult is it for you to say no?										
How much do you need to be in control of situations?										
How much does your personal appearance matter to you?										

2. What expectation do you place on yourself to make yourself acceptable?

3. When people meet you, what impression do you think they have of you?

4. How does what others perceive about you compare to what you are really feeling on the inside?

SESSION 7: SMALL GROUP QUESTIONS

- What are the expectations that you place on yourself to make yourself acceptable?

- What things do you do to find approval from others?

- What are the expectations that society, family or peers place upon you to make you acceptable to them?

- Have you created a false image based on your own expectations?

> *"You will never feel worthy of others' acceptance until you can actually love and accept yourself."*

SECTION 7: PERSONAL MINISTRY EXERCISE

DESTROYING THE FALSE IDENTITY AND RESTORING YOUR TRUE IDENTITY

1. **EXPLANATION:** In this section you will work on removing the obstacles that keep you from walking in God's original design for your identity. As a result of shame, which destroys your God-given identity, a false image has been designed to give you value, worth, and significance. However the DNA of this false image (self idol) was created from your shame and love deficit, thus its fruit will not bring you the inner joy and fulfillment you seek.

   The false image (self-idol) is made up of the expectations you believed you needed to become acceptable to God, others, and ultimately yourself. This idol acts as a barrier keeping you from receiving the grace and love you long for. Therefore, this self-idol needs to be brought down.

2. **REFLECTION:** Take a moment and ask the Holy Spirit what your self-idol looks like in your heart. Then in the box below draw or describe what it looks or feels like to you. On the right, list the various expectations that you need to live up to in order to meet the requirements of this "idol".

MY SELF IDOL	EXPECTATIONS (Perfectionism, status, recognition etc.)

3. **APPLICATION:** Now that you have identified the make up of your false image, it is important that you remove it. The scriptures are clear that we are to have no other gods before our God (Exodus 20:3-6). Therefore it is vital that we tear down the idol of self and release ourselves from its requirements of us.

Before you pray the following prayer, imagine your idol in your mind and ask Jesus what He wants you to do with it. Listen to the first thing that comes to you. Take the idol in your mind and imagine yourself doing whatever you felt Jesus tell you to do. For example, if you are to crush it, then see yourself grinding it in your hands or crushing it with your feet until it becomes dust; or if you are to throw it away, then hurl it as far as you can from you until it disappears.

Then pray the following prayer:

PRAYER TO TEAR DOWN MY SELF-IDOL

Lord Jesus,

I declare that You are my Lord, my Savior and my Redeemer. You are my God and I agree with Your Word that I am to have no other gods before You. I repent for creating and serving my false image (idol) in the hope that it would bring blessing to my life. I confess that I tried to find value, worth and significance by trying to meet the expectations of my idol – by creating a righteousness of my own. As a result, I recognize that I rejected Your grace and workmanship in my life by building my own self-image and identity. Therefore, I repent for the glory that I gained for myself as a result of my success and performance. I realise now that I misused the gifting, anointing and calling that You gave me to give glory to myself and not to You.

So, by an act of my will I tear down and destroy this idol from my life. I understand, that it does not remove my shame, but keeps me a captive to the lies that bind me. Forgive me for giving myself the highest place in my life. I now surrender again all that I am for Your glory alone. Thank You for releasing Your grace and forgiveness into my life.

In Jesus' name,

Amen.

4. **MINISTRY EXERCISE #2(a):** Having torn down your self-idol, it is time to deal with the lies that caused the idol to be created. Hiding behind the idol is the part of you that you believed was not acceptable. It represents the shame that was put on you, and that you agreed with.

   For a moment, pray and ask the Holy Spirit to show you an image of your inner-self that was hiding behind the idol. Then in the box below draw or describe what you see or how it feels to you. On the right side, list the negative "I am..." statements that you have agreed with (e.g. I am not good enough; I am disqualified etc.) You may want to refer to your Identity Tree worksheet from the Personal Ministry Experience for Session 6, page 53.

MY INNER SELF	MY "I AM..." AGREEMENTS

5. **MINISTRY EXERCISE #2(b):** Before you can break these negative agreements, it is vital that you know how God sees you. It is important that you replace those lies with God's truth. The following exercise is designed for you to listen to His still, small voice. It is important that as you go through this ministry exercise, you relax and try not to overthink or anticipate what the correct answers are. This is not about right or wrong answers, but about God wanting to speak His unique affection towards you.

   Before we start this exercise, pray the following prayer:

PRAYER TO PREPARE THE HEART TO HEAR GOD'S VOICE

Lord Jesus,

Thank You that You are the Good Shepherd, and You long for me to know and hear Your voice. Therefore, I cast aside everything that keeps me from discerning Your still, small voice. Fill me with the peace that transcends all understanding and grant me a spirit of wisdom and revelation to receive the truth of what You are speaking lovingly to me. Quiet my soul, Lord Jesus, and, Holy Spirit of truth, lead me into all truth- the truth that will set me free.

I pray this in Jesus' name,

Amen.

6. **APPLICATION:** Now, take a moment to pray and ask the Jesus the following questions. In the spaces that follow, write or draw the impressions or words that flow into your heart. Listen to the first thing that comes to your heart - don't dismiss it. Sometimes what we first sense seems simple. However, as the exercise progresses, what you might think is simple, can become profound and transformative.

QUESTION 1: LORD JESUS, WHEN YOU LOOK AT ME, WHO AM I TO YOU?

QUESTION 2: WHY DO YOU SEE ME THIS WAY?

Copyright Steve Chua: Seek First International 2014   *www.stevechua.net*

QUESTION 3: WHAT ARE YOUR THOUGHTS TOWARDS ME IN THIS MOMENT?

QUESTION 4: WHAT IS YOUR DESIRE FOR ME IN THIS MOMENT?

QUESTION 5: IF I WERE TO BELIEVE EVERYTHING THAT HAS JUST BEEN REVEALED TO ME, HOW WOULD THAT CHANGE MY LIFE?

QUESTION 6: WHY HAS THE ENEMY SPENT SO MUCH TIME TRYING TO DESTROY WHO I AM? WHY IS HE AFRAID OF ME?

If what has been revealed to you is positive and life-giving, then it's time to decide whether you want to agree with God and what He says about you, or to continue believing what Satan has led you to believe. If you desire to break your agreements with the enemy's lies, pray the following prayer from your heart.

PRAYER TO BREAK AGREEMENTS WITH YOUR SHAME

Dear Lord Jesus,

Thank You that You are the way, the truth and the life. Thank You that You have come to set me free from the curse of my shame. I confess that I have agreed with the enemy's lies, and through the power of my agreements I have been rejecting the identity and destiny that You created for me.

I now break my agreements with the following lies _____(Verbally renounce all the negative shame statements you have listed on p.66) and release myself from all the following false responsibilities and expectations that I have placed on myself: _____(Verbally renounce all expectations you have listed on p.64)

I declare to the enemy that you no longer have any rights over me and that every negative influence and curse that has been in operation over my identity is broken in the name of Jesus.

I declare that I am God's child and that He says that I am _____ (Verbally declare what Jesus revealed to you on p.68-70). I now choose to take His word and place it back into my heart. From this day on I live free of my past shame and walk into my future. I declare that God has plans for me, to prosper me not to harm me, to give me a hope and a future.

Thank you, Jesus, that You have forgiven my sin and cleansed my shame. Thank You that You love me and that I am priceless in Your eyes. I receive the grace You won for me, so I can be free to be who You created me to be. From this day on I choose to live for Your glory and not my own.

I pray and declare this in the wonderful name of Jesus.

Amen.

7. **FINAL APPLICATION:** If you are doing this exercise in a small group setting, find a partner and take a moment to share the words that you have received. If you are listening to another's testimony and what you are hearing is positive and life giving, take a moment to affirm and pray for your partner. Pray and bless the personal revelation received and ask the Lord to establish and root that word into the heart of one another.

A FINAL BLESSING FROM STEVE CHUA

I pray that this journey to discover your true identity has brought you great revelation and personal freedom. In the coming days, take time to ponder what God has revealed to you about your pricelessness. Since the beginning of time, He has loved you and longs for you to know your inheritance and identity as His child. You no longer have to live with an orphan heart, which always feels rejected and deprived. But as a child of God, you can live from a place of security and confidence, knowing that you are unconditionally loved. This revelation will become the launching pad for you to discover the destiny that God has for you.

As you walk out your healing, you will discover that you now have the ability to freely choose how to respond to circumstances and relationships. Old patterns will want to creep back, but you no longer have to live with the lies the enemy had sown into your heart. Each day you can walk in greater freedom. In addition, I encourage you to look for a community that can help you with your journey. We were created for relationship, so healing is best worked out in a place of safe and encouraging community and friendship.

Finally, I want to bless you with the Father's blessing that you would know all that He has created and purposed for you, and that you can walk in the fullness of your inheritance as His child. I pray that you will know that every blessing in the heavenly realm is available to you (Ephesians 1:3) and that His plans are to prosper you and to give you a hope and an amazing future (Jeremiah 29:11). As you continue to walk with Him, may you daily be in awe of His grace and may you begin to comprehend the height, depth, length and width of His abundant love for you (Ephesians 3:18).

With much love and blessings,

STEVE CHUA